Leg

MW01296476

First Printing: 2012

ISBN-13: 978-1479144167

ISBN-10: 1479144169

Printed in the United States of America

Table of Contents

Introduction 1

My Background 2

When Will the Phone Ring? 3

Never Leave Home Without It 4

He Who Does Not Ask a Question Remains a Fool Forever
(Chinese Proverb) 5

Making the Classroom Student-Proof 7

The Substitute's Morning Upheaval 9

Expectations 11

Uh Oh! 13

To the Blackboard or To the Office 15

The Boy in the Bathroom 17

What You Need – Just In Case 18

The Eyes Have It.. 20

Let's Do It Again 21

Conclusion 22

Ideas for Activities 23

Meet Elizabeth Reynolds 25

Dedication

To Kelly and Stefanie

Two Very Special Young Women

Introduction

How do you handle walking into a school as a substitute teacher for the first time when you don't know anything about the school, its specific rules, the class you'll be teaching, or even if the regular teacher has left you a lesson plan? What do you do when you first get to the classroom? How do you handle meeting the students? Are they really as monstrous to subs as you've heard and if so, how do you deal with them? What if any materials do you need to bring with you?

This book will answer all those questions and more. It is designed primarily for those who are new to substitute teaching. My purpose in writing it is to give you practical pointers and suggestions so your first experiences as a sub will be better than mine were, and you can learn from my initial experiences. If you're an experienced sub, you may also benefit from this book. You may pick up tips you hadn't thought of, and you may get some ideas for activities and ways to discipline students, which we as subs can always use.

When I share my tips, I'll describe some of the difficulties I encountered as a sub so you'll understand why I'm giving you that particular advice. At the end of the book I'll list some ideas I've developed or come across for activities. I'll also give you websites where you can go to print pages for additional activities.

This book is intended to be a guide primarily for elementary school substitutes, although some of the suggestions may pertain to high school as well. Unlike many school districts which only go through 5th or 6th grade, Chicago's elementary school district goes through 8th grade, so the experiences I talk about cover all those grades.

My Background

First let me give you a little background about myself. I received an undergraduate degree in elementary education almost 40 years ago. However, instead of teaching full-time, I changed my career course, pursued an MBA degree, and spent my career in a corporate environment. I did however substitute teach for a while in a private religious school in Chicago.

When I was in my late 50s, I was laid off from my corporate job. This was at the end of 2008 when it seemed as if everyone was being laid off, and it was pretty much impossible to find another job. So I decided to renew my teaching certificate and substitute teach until I retire. I fulfilled the necessary requirements to renew my certificate, submitted all the paperwork, and excitedly – and naively - got ready for my first day of substitute teaching in the Chicago public schools.

I expected my new subbing experiences to be just like my previous ones. Well, they couldn't have been more different. Whether it was because of different school systems, the passing of time, or a generation of bolder and more precocious children, things had definitely changed.

So let's begin.

When Will the Phone Ring?

Just because you're ready to sub, doesn't mean the school district is ready to call you. This is especially true at the beginning of the school year. In my experience, it's unusual for a lot of teachers to call in sick or to need a personal day early in the school year. Just because you're ready to go to work, that doesn't mean there will be a great need for subs right away. You may be up and ready for that phone call, but it won't necessarily come. Take heart; eventually the phone will start ringing. It did with me, and to my delight, it hasn't stopped. There are even a couple of schools that wanted to put me on their sub lists. That means that I am among the first to be called if they need a sub. There are even times I know in advance that I have a job for a certain day.

Never Leave Home Without It

There are certain supplies you should bring with you every time you go to a school. The reasons why, and how you should use them will be explained during your reading of this book. You should always have with you:

Adhesive tape

Sharpie®

Plain paper cut into strips about 4" x 10"

Word search sheets

Riddles

Pictures to color

Books to read to the students

Ideas for games to play

Pen and paper

Pencils

Band-aids®

He Who Does Not Ask a Question Remains a Fool Forever (Chinese Proverb)

So what is it like to walk into a school for the first time as a sub? It can be very daunting. Not only does every school have its own rules, every teacher has her own rules. You don't know what you're walking into until you're there.

Additionally, you may have some students in your class who have special needs and schedules that are different from the rest of the class. It's good to know this in advance so you can keep track of those students and where they're supposed to go.

So here we have my next piece of advice. When you check in at the school office, ask questions.

Ask if any students have special needs or special schedules. If the office staff doesn't know this, they should be able to give you the name of another teacher you can ask. It's usually a teacher of the same grade in a classroom close to yours.

Also ask about the school's rules, particularly the bathroom rules.

Let me repeat this. *Particularly the bathroom rules.*

Regardless of the grade in which you are subbing, your students will try to take advantage of bathroom breaks. Often, the bathroom breaks are scheduled occurrences – one in the morning and one in the afternoon, but in some schools teachers let the students go to the bathroom whenever they need to. If your school falls into the first category, be assured your students, especially the younger ones, will try to get around the schedule by constantly repeating that they can't hold it. They're using this as a test to see how much they can get away with in your classroom.

One first grader continually said to me, "Please, please can I go to the bathroom? I can't hold it. I can't hold it." Of course he didn't just say this. He acted it out, with groans and his hands in the proper place to indicate he couldn't hold it. I hadn't asked about the rules for allowing students to go to the bathroom, and this boy had me completely fooled. I let him go. So wouldn't you know it, all of a sudden, none of the kids could hold it!

If you know the school's rules – and stick to them – you're in a much better position not to be taken advantage of. If a child comes up to you and acts the way my first grader did, just tell him the school has a rule about bathroom breaks and he can't go until the scheduled time. You may have to repeat this a few times, especially with the little ones, but eventually they'll get the message. They'll see that they can't take advantage of you.

Making the Classroom Student-Proof

As soon as you walk into the room, hide the chalk and erasers! When kids line up, whether it's for gym, recess, lunch or end-of-day dismissal, if they are standing near the blackboard, they will grab the chalk and start drawing. It's as if they are chalk magnets! Not only will they draw, if they really want to get you going, they will erase what you've written!

You may think that in this age of computers and technology, there are no more blackboards and chalk. Well, the same applies for whiteboards and markers. All I can say is keep them out of sight, and you'll be better off.

Students also love to flip the switch on an overhead projector. (Yes, some classrooms still use those.) Your best bet is to move it to a corner, as far away as possible from where the students will be lining up.

Next, take a look at the student roster. You're going to spend a good part of the day with these kids. If your memory is as bad as mine or if you have 25-plus kids in your class, you'll need some help remembering who's who. Take the strips of paper I suggested you bring and write every student's name with the Sharpie® I put on the list (so it's easily visible from a distance) on a separate strip. Then tape it to their desk with the adhesive tape in a place where you can easily see it. If you don't know where the children are sitting before they come in, do it after you've taken attendance.

I was a co-substitute with another teacher in a kindergarten class. He didn't bother to learn the children's names. Instead, he would address them as "boy in the blue shirt" or "girl with the ponytail." He didn't care at all about establishing a rapport with the students, and they knew it. Kindergarteners can be so warm and friendly, even to substitute teachers. They're too young to have learned they're not supposed to like subs. This man's laziness in terms of not learning the students' names resulted in their not paying any attention to him and not showing any openness toward him. It was such a shame to see this.

Be sure to write your name on the blackboard. I learned from colleagues that if you have a last name that is difficult to read or pronounce, it can be better to just use your first initial. This is especially true if you're going to be with primary grade students.

Don't forget to take the time to review the fire and emergency evacuation plans. They should be located on the classroom wall.

The Substitute's Morning Upheaval

Okay. Now you're ready to greet your class.

It's a good idea to take some time to introduce yourself to your students when you first meet them and to learn who they are. If you have time for this, by all means do it. Tell the students your name, why you're there, ask them their names, etc. However at many of the schools where I sub, the first part of the day is very hectic. There are announcements coming over the PA system; I have to take attendance while students are hanging up their coats and making lots of noise; the pledge of allegiance comes over the PA system; and I have to collect lunch money – all before the first bell. So all I have time to do is tell them my name and that I'm substituting for their regular teacher. Also each school has a different system for handling this time. You don't know what you're walking into beforehand.

So here's my next tip. Don't get frazzled during these moments. Things will settle down.

You can make it easier on yourself by asking a student to be your assistant for the collection of lunch money and taking attendance. A great job for a student helper is the collection of homework, which some regular teachers ask their substitutes to do first thing in the morning.

A student assistant can be particularly helpful with attendance. If you're not sure how to pronounce a child's name, ask your helper. You'll save yourself embarrassment and avoid laughter and/or unruly behavior among the students if you don't mispronounce a child's name.

Using a student helper for the collection of lunch money can be a smart move as well. In just one classroom you may have students who get free lunch, those who pay the full amount for lunch, those who pay a partial amount and students who buy only milk. When you collect lunch money from the students, they assume you know which category they fall into. Additionally, some of them are bringing extra money because they owe from a previous day. Some may have brought too much and they're going to want change, expecting that you'll know exactly how much they should get. An assistant can help you handle all of this, and collecting lunch money will run much more efficiently with his or her help.

Don't ask for volunteers. All the students will raise their hands. Pick someone to help you. It goes much more smoothly that way. Some regular teachers assign a different student to be a helper each week. If this is the case in your classroom, pick that student to be your assistant. You can usually find the list of helpers posted on the wall.

By the way, I've actually been in classrooms where I couldn't find a pen or pencil to use for taking attendance. Hard to believe, but it's true. That's why I recommend bringing your own.

Expectations

After you've gone through the morning routine, it's time to introduce yourself. By this I mean, go over your own rules.

Tell the students you expect them to follow the same rules that they follow for their regular teacher (including the all-important bathroom rules). Be quiet in class and in the hallways, be respectful, work quietly, raise your hand.

It's important that you stick to this too; otherwise they won't behave for you at all. For instance, if you tell them you expect them to be quiet in the hall on the way to the lunchroom, bring them back to the classroom if they're too noisy or rambunctious. I always hate to do this because it cuts into my short lunch time as well as theirs, but it is necessary if they're going to understand that I'm serious.

Your students will spend a good part of the day telling you how they "always" do things. When it comes to certain routines, it's good to try not to change them, especially with younger students. They prefer that their routines not be altered, and if you change them, they will tell you that you're not doing it the way their teacher does it. This goes for the time of day they eat their snacks, discussing the day's date and weather, writing the date on the blackboard, the order in which each subject's lesson is taught, just about everything they do. They're used to a certain routine, and they expect it to continue with you.

The regular teacher will outline many of the routines in the information left for you, such as if you should take the students to the lunchroom and if you should pick them up, if you should take them to gym and pick them up, and where to deliver them at the end of the day to either meet their parents or get on their buses. However, she may not mention how she has them line up (for instance boys in one line and girls in another, alphabetically, or those exhibiting good behavior go first). If you do it differently than she does, the students will be sure to let you know. In those cases, it's best to ask one student in advance how the teacher does it.

Students may also tell you certain things that aren't true simply because you're the substitute. Again they'll be trying to take advantage of you. For instance, they may tell you that their regular teacher allows them to move their desks around or change their seats. I have never found this to be true. If you allow the students to move their desks, it creates chaos in the classroom. If you allow them to change seats, they do it to sit next to their friends. The end result is a noisy classroom where they're not paying attention. Let them know that their teacher didn't leave instructions for you about this, so you're not going to permit it.

Uh Oh!

So now you've gotten through the morning routine and you've gone over your own rules. Now it's time to get down to actually teaching your class. This is where my next tip comes in. If you're a new substitute, don't expect perfection.

Let me tell you what happened on my first day of subbing. It had been years since I was in a classroom, so I was nervous but also excited. How tough could it be? A lot of years had passed sure, but that also meant I was more experienced in life. I could handle the students and anything they would throw at me, correct? Well, not correct – at least not right away. But each experience taught me how to handle it the next time. I'll share some of those experiences with you now, so that you can learn from my missteps.

I was assigned to a large third grade class. Immediately, one of the little girls decided she was going to be my helper. Any time I did something the least bit differently from her regular teacher, she popped out of her seat and told me how it should be done. (That's when I came up with the idea of going over my own rules.)

The worst part came in the afternoon. After I had escorted the kids back to the classroom from the lunchroom, I noticed I had one less student. After they were seated in class, I noticed that Kevin was missing. (I actually was pretty proud of myself for noticing that one of the children was missing.) So I asked, "Where's Kevin?" All of a sudden, my little 8-year-old helper stands up and shouts at the top of her voice, "We have a child missing!" I was wondering, "Who's in charge of this class? You or me?" Of course, that thought only occurred to me when I wasn't panicking about having lost Kevin. Not a good thing to have happen to you on your first day of subbing.

It ended up all right – after what seemed to me like a very long time. I sent two students to a neighboring teacher to ask if she knew where Kevin might be. They returned with the information that Kevin had a class with a different teacher after lunch. Since he always went there, it never occurred to him to tell me - not that he would have anyway. (That's when I learned to ask questions upon arrival at the school.)

There were other times I wondered what I had gotten myself into. When I entered a classroom at another school, the teacher was actually there. Even though she didn't plan on teaching that day, she came in to meet with the parent of one of her third grade students. That's because on the previous day, that student had stabbed another child with a pencil! By this time I had subbed enough to know the discipline problems that substitutes can encounter. I thought, if this is the type of problem the regular teacher has, what am *I* going to run into at this school? I learned not to accept assignments at certain schools because the discipline problems were just too much to handle.

There are other schools where the students are very well-behaved and self-motivated, and I'm always glad to get calls to go to those schools. Most of the schools are somewhere in between these two extremes. The classes I'm assigned to have mostly well-behaved students, but there are always a few who have decided it's their duty to challenge the substitute. A 7th grader once asked me how long I had been married and when I said 25 years, she asked, "Is he still hot for your body?" That's when I learned to not answer any personal questions. But I had to answer the question the first time before I learned not to do it again. As I said, don't expect perfection from yourself. It takes time to learn how to deal with students who are trying to get the better of a substitute. Understand that you will make mistakes. Every substitute does. It's a process, and you'll learn from it.

To the Blackboard or To the Office?

This is a good place to discuss tips for disciplining students. Every class has some terrific, self-motivated, well-behaved students. On the other hand, every class also has those whose goal for the day is to see how much they can get away with. You'd better get used to it; it comes with the territory. There are a few things you can do to make it easier on yourself. Don't expect to solve the problem completely – that's impossible for a sub – but you can improve the situation.

I found one of the best techniques is to offer the students a reward for good behavior. Kids love to play games, and if you promise them a game at the end of the day for behaving well, that goes a long way toward achieving the behavior you want.

There has to be a consequence for bad behavior though, so here's what I do. I write on the board, "We will play a game at 2:45." Each time someone misbehaves, I erase one number or letter. I tell the students that if the entire sentence is erased, there will be no game. That helps to keep them in line.

Kids also want their regular teacher to know if they behave well. I tell them that at the end of the day I will put a list of the best-behaved students on the board for their teacher to see the next day. I call the list Mrs. R's Superstars.

Originally I put the list up early in the day and added to it throughout the day. I discovered this didn't work. There would always be someone asking why he/she didn't get on the list or why someone else did. So I save it for the end of the day, and it provides more of a goal to work toward.

Another technique is to divide the class into groups with points awarded for good behavior during specified periods of time. Toward the end of the day, the group with the most points gets a reward, such as time to read, color or work on the computers (depending on the grade).

Students in the upper grades love to get a jump on their homework. That can be used as an incentive as well.

There may be times when you have no choice but to send a child to the office. If the student gets so out of hand that you can't deal with him, by all means do so. There are those times when a fight breaks out, and sending a child to the office is your only option. Don't feel bad; this probably happens to all subs at one time or another.

Classroom management and discipline will get easier for you as you gain experience. You will learn what works and what doesn't work for you and your personality.

The Boy in the Bathroom

As the only adult in the room, it is your responsibility to monitor all the students. However, there are times when one of the children needs to leave the room. You may need to ask a student to take attendance forms or notes from parents to the office; a student may be sick and need to see the nurse; or the bathroom rules may be such that a student may be allowed to leave the room whenever he or she needs to go.

I have found it is best to never let a student leave your sight unaccompanied. Always use the buddy system. Send two students together. When a student is in the hall alone, anything can happen (and often does). A corollary to this advice is if you think one of the students might not be particularly well-behaved, make sure the buddy isn't one of his good friends.

I substituted in a 6th grade class that allowed students to go to the bathroom whenever they needed to. I allowed one boy to go by himself. I continued helping the rest of the students work individually on math problems. After about five minutes, I realized the boy hadn't returned. Not being able to leave the classroom myself, I sent another boy after him. Well, that student didn't return either! I started to wonder, was I living my own version of the Twilight Zone, where kids got sucked down a toilet never to be seen again? That's when the buddy system, and more importantly, its corollary would have been good tips to have known.

I chose a boy I knew to be responsible and sent him to see what happened to the first two. He returned and told me they were roughhousing in the bathroom. Since I couldn't leave, he became my messenger. I had him make it very clear to the two boys that their next trip would be to the office if they didn't return immediately. There are times when threats of being sent to the office work wonders!

What You Need – Just In Case

Some teachers are terrific about leaving lesson plans; some aren't. If you walk into a classroom and there's no plan for how you should spend the day with the students, what do you do?

Some teachers don't know until they get up in the morning that they won't be in, and they therefore have to put together lesson plans and email them to the school. What do you do in the meantime?

Even if your teacher leaves a comprehensive lesson plan, you may finish the lesson before the period is over. Then what do you do?

The answer to all these questions is the same, and it's my next piece of advice. Bring enough materials to handle any situation.

I call these "just in case" materials. They include word search sheets, riddles, pictures to color, books to read to the class, and ideas for activities. Also, because you may not know in advance what grade you'll be teaching (I never do), you need to bring enough to cover all grades. Kindergarteners love to color. Sixth graders love to do word searches. Yes, it's a lot to carry, but believe me, it's worth it to have enough to keep the students busy.

Kids of various ages seem to enjoy a book called <u>No More Homework! No More Tests! Kids Favorite Funny School Poems</u> with poems selected by Bruce Lansky. Kindergarteners enjoy hearing me read Shel Silverstein's <u>The Giving Tree</u>. Afterward they like to color a picture of a tree.

I also include in this category materials that the students should have but don't. On more occasions than I can mention, students don't have pencils to do their work. I have often suggested they borrow one from a fellow student, but many times another student doesn't have one to loan them.

You can save a lot of time by having extra pencils of your own to hand out. Just be sure to make a note of which students you gave them to and collect them at the end of the day.

Once when I was subbing for a 4th grade class, a boy came up to me looking very frustrated. He pointed to another boy holding a pencil and said, "Mark won't give me that pencil." I asked the boy if the pencil was his. He said, "No, but I want to use it." I don't know why he felt entitled to use another child's pencil, but I easily resolved the issue by lending him one of mine.

Also on my list is Band-Aids®. If you don't want your students asking to go to the nurse to get a bandage for every little scratch, carry a supply with you.

The Eyes Have It

I'm going to tell you now about my next tip, but it's one I've yet to master. Have eyes in the back of your head. I'll give you an example from my own subbing experience.

A teacher for a first grade class I was subbing for left instructions for an art project she wanted the children to work on. They were supposed to cut out forms from construction paper and glue them onto other larger white paper. Twenty-five kids and glue is a bad combination. While I was helping other students, one of the boys spilled glue on his desk. When little boys spill glue, they don't just spill a small amount. This particular little boy decided to "clean up" the glue with Kleenex®. Needless to say, he ended up with a nice pile of Kleenex® stuck to his desk.

Let's Do It Again

There are several things you can do to leave a good impression so that the regular teacher will want you to substitute for her again.

Students tend to leave papers, pencils, crayons, tissues and the occasional book on the floor. Also they tend to leave their desks and chairs in a disorderly arrangement. Before students are dismissed, have them pick up everything on the floor around their desks, throw away the trash, and straighten up their desks and chairs. After they have left, pick up anything they may have missed. Strictly speaking this isn't your job, but the regular teacher will return to a neat room, and you'll get more points than if the teacher returns to a messy room.

At the end of the day, leave a note for the regular teacher, discussing how much of the lesson plans you covered. (This is why I suggested that you bring paper.) Mention any areas of the lessons you feel the students had trouble with. Also let the teacher know any positives that happened during the day, including names of particularly well-behaved students. Also let her know who the troublemakers were and what, if any, disciplinary action was taken. Don't leave the teacher in the dark. She'll appreciate having this information.

Conclusion

In this book, I gave you suggestions for handling your day as a substitute teacher. A lot of this might sound overwhelming, and it probably sounds like the day is grueling. To tell you the truth, it can be difficult at the beginning. But after that, it can be great. Of course, a lot depends on the school you are assigned to and the particular class within the school; but there can be some great times when you're not just a babysitter. Sometimes you can put your teaching skills to good use. And when you see a student grasp a concept you've taught, or when a 5-year old gives you a hug, or when one of the students waves and says hello to you the next time you're at that school, it can feel really terrific. My tips are meant to get you to that point a little sooner than you'd get there on your own.

Ideas for Activities

Games

I've found that students enjoy the following games.

Heads Up, Seven Up is a very popular game among younger students. Here's a description in a nutshell. The teacher picks seven students to come to the front of the class. Everyone else is told to put their heads down and close their eyes. The seven students each secretly tap one person on the shoulder and return to the front of the classroom. The teacher then calls," heads up seven up." The seven kids who were tapped on the shoulder stand up and try to guess who tapped them. If they guess correctly, the person who tapped them sits down and the successful guesser takes their place. If they guess incorrectly, they sit down again. After all the standing students have tried to guess who tapped them, the students at the front of the class tell who they picked. The game then starts again.

You're probably familiar with Hangman, the game where one person thinks of a word and the other players attempt to figure it out by guessing which letters belong in the word. I usually play this game using words from the students' spelling, science or social studies lessons.

In a variation on this game, I put words from the students' lessons on the board with just two or three letters missing (depending on the length of the word). I have the students identify the word by guessing the missing letters.

Online Resources

There are many online resources for worksheets you can print and hand out to your students. I've listed just a few of them here.

Crayola

http://www.crayola.com/

and

Coloring Pages for Kids

http://www.coloring-pages-kids.com/

Free coloring pages to print for students. There are a variety of categories to choose from, such as animals and holidays.

TLSBooks.com

http://www.tlsbooks.com/

Free worksheets on all elementary school subjects by grade. Also coloring pages and word search sheets.

Puzzle Choice

http://www.puzzlechoice.com/pc/Puzzle_Choicex.html

Free crossword puzzles, word search puzzles, brainteasers, and more.

Meet Elizabeth Reynolds

Hi! I'm Elizabeth Reynolds, author of Are You Ready to Be a Substitute Teacher? Practical Tips for Keeping Your Sanity.

I have been both a business woman and an educator, most recently substitute teaching in Chicago's public schools.

Working as a substitute has been fun, rewarding, annoying and wearisome – sometimes all in the same day. I hope this book will enable you to find more of the positives and less of the negatives that can accompany the job of substitute teacher.

Made in the USA
Lexington, KY
07 October 2012